D1502815

RAY J. ALTHOFF

CARL PHILLIPS

DOUBLE SHADOW

Carl Phillips is the author of ten previous books
of poems, including *Speak Low*, a finalist for the
National Book Award, and *Quiver of Arrows:
Selected Poems, 1986–2006*. He teaches at
Washington University in St. Louis.

DOUBLE SHADOW

DOUBLE

FARRAR STRAUS GIROUX NEW YORK

SHADOW

CARL PHILLIPS

FARRAR, STRAUS AND GIROUX

18 West 18th Street, New York 10011

Distributed in Canada by D&M Publishers, Inc.

Printed in the United States of America

Published in 2011 by Farrar, Straus and Giroux

First paperback edition, 2012

The Library of Congress has cataloged

the hardcover edition as follows:

Phillips, Carl, 1959–

  Double shadow / Carl Phillips. — 1st ed.

    p. cm.

  ISBN 978-0-374-14157-8 (alk. paper)

  I. Title.

PS3566.H476 D68 2011

813'.54 — dc22

2010033097

Paperback ISBN: 978-0-374-53315-1

Designed by Quemadura

www.fsgbooks.com

1 3 5 7 9 10 8 6 4 2

"Look," the ocean said *(it was tumbled, like our sheets), "look in my eyes"*

JAMES SCHUYLER

CONTENTS

*

DOUBLE SHADOW

FIRST NIGHT AT SEA

Like any other kingdom built of wickedness and
joy—cracked, anchorless, bit of ghost in the making,
only here for now. Blue for once not just as in
forgive, but blue as blue . . . As affection was never

twilight, but a light of its own, blindness not at all
a gift to be held close to the chest, stubborn horse
meanwhile beating wild beneath it, stubborn heart,
a dark, where was a brightness, a bright where dark.

RANSOM

How he was carried in a ramshackle cart alongside the sea.
How he lay on his side, on a bed of straw—
mules pulling the cart; the straw
for the blood . . . So it isn't true, even in reverse,
that I have no memory or that I felt no loss or a kind
of sorrow, or I have felt none since. The sea, as in
that underworld that mostly the mind resembles. Blood,
not as in power but the echo of it, and the echo fading—
fog as it lifts, delusion-like, *come*
clean again, from a thicket all thorns . . . And how the stars
swelled the dark, guiding the man whose whip
made the mules go faster, though they would have
run, I think, even had there been no whip, being mules, and
broken long ago, and with no more belief than disbelief in rescue.

NEXT STOP, ARCADIA

There's a man asking to be worshipped only.
He looks inconsolable; rugged; like those
once-popular, but hardly seen anymore
portraits—depictions, really—of Jesus.
There's another man. He wants to be
flogged while naked and on all fours—
begging for it; no mercy; he says *Make me
beg.*
      There's a field nearby. Stretch of field—
like the one they say divides prayer from
absolute defeat. Here's where the packhorse,
scaring at nothing visible, broke its tether;
no sign of it since. You know this field:
a constant stirring inside an otherwise great
stillness that never stops surrounding it,
the way memory doesn't, though memory
is not just a stillness,
                but a field that stirs.
The two men—they've gone nowhere.

They've got questions. Like *Which one's*
the field you can actually remember? and
Which one's the one you're only imagining
now—standing inside it, staying there,
stay,

       until it looks like home? Who are they,
to be asking questions? You look from one man
to the other. You keep looking—but between
submission, or the seeming resistance that
more often than not, lately, comes just
before it,

       which is better? It's hard to decide:
the ugliness of weeping, or the tears themselves?

FASCINATION

Guttering in its stone urn from a century, by now,
too far away, the candle made of the room
a cavernousness. The shape of the light getting cast
upward, onto the room's ceiling, became a kind
of moon, some
                        overlooked, last round of desire—
unclaimed, searching . . .

                                *

                        There are places, still, that
no moonlight ever quite conquers: a thickness of brush,
the crossed limbs of cathedral pines,
                                defend the dark,
inside which—beneath it—the trapped fox has stopped
mutilating its own body to at last get free. Has stopped trying.
Consigns the rust-colored full length of itself to the frosted ground.

SKY COMING FORWARD

How the birches sway, for example. How they
tilt, on occasion, their made-to-tilt-by-the-wind
crowns. How by then he had turned his head
away, as if a little in fear; or shy, maybe . . . Also
the leaves having stopped their falling. Or there
were no leaves left—left to fall. Which to call
more true? Love

          or mercy? Both of his hands
upraised, but the better of the two tipped more
groundward, the other a lone bird lifting, as if from
a wood gone steep with twilight. Sometimes, an
abrupt yet gentle breaking of the storm

                          inside me:
for a moment, just the rings that form then disappear
around where some latest desire—lost, or abandoned—
dropped once, and disturbed the water. To forget—
then remember . . . What if, between this one and the one
we hoped for, there's a third life, taking its own
slow, dreamlike hold, even now—blooming, in spite of us?

CONTINUOUS UNTIL WE STOP

But when I came to what I'd been told
was the zone of tragedy—transition—it was
not that. Was a wildering field, across it the light
steadily lessening, and the tall grasses, waving,
deepened their colors: blue-green, or
a greenish blue . . . hard to tell, exactly. Was like
when the body surrenders to risk, that moment
when an unwillingness to refuse can seem

no different from an inability to,
though they are not the same—inability,
unwillingness. To have said otherwise
doesn't make it true, or even make it count
as true. Yes, but what does the truth
matter now, I whispered, stepping further inside what,
by then, was night, almost. The tamer animals
would soon lie down again, and the wild go free.

THE GRASS NOT BEING FLESH,
NOR FLESH THE GRASS

Like one of those moths, palpable
just to look at, but as if weightless as dust,
colorless
        as dust, landing on the sleeper's
mouth in the dream of darkness—and then the dark,
for real—he came to me. *Rest*, I said; and for many years,
between love and a way of loving—for they are not
the same—it is true,
        he did rest. Fluttering moth, all the more
attractive for the torn, the battered parts. As with
the others before, and since then. Him turning, or
sometimes
        I did: birch leaves when, in a gust of storm,
they'll show the side that's silver, in the same way that
certain hard mistakes do, though less
unexpectedly. Aren't they
        always fluttering? *Rest*, I say,
each night—to each of them. And in the dream, I'm resting.

THE HEAT OF THE SUN

Calming the bell was nothing easy. Nor did
the calmness, after, make the air surrounding it—
though at first it had seemed to—any more
still,
      or clear. The usual clouds building up
into shapes I almost recognized, and then
letting go of them. Customs like the breaking
in two of willow branches, which maybe still
stands for parting, somewhere. Maybe the mistake
of hoping
          never to make mistakes is the only
pattern we get to leave behind us: no bells—just
a calmness, after; the air so clear, we forget what
hurt so much and, in forgetting it, think it's disappeared.

THROUGH AN OPENING

It was as if they'd stepped into the head
of a wind god
          and gotten trapped there and,
within captivity, made a space they could

sometimes recognize. Soon it looked
like home: chicken hawk; first stars;
a golden steeple . . . Almost, they could believe
each word of it,

          the wordless parts also,
the particular riot—and beauty, for they did
admit as much—of a field on fire, the wind
tumbling through the god's hair, here and

there lifting it—so a kind of life, still—
They would make
          a music of it. Singing
Hush now—why not hush? You're mine, coyote.

AFTER THE THUNDER,
BEFORE THE RAIN

Cicadas, or locusts—by whatever name, they've at last
gone silent, like suitors outmatched by what the body can
sometimes ask for and, other times, require. You've said
what you've said. So have I. What I think I meant, though,
was not guilt, but humility: being able to see—to recognize—
a failure that belongs, finally, not so much to the dream as
to the dreamer. As if that

matters, now . . . Neither viciousness
nor the right kind of love, if there even is such a place. Not
abandon, but no harm, or less of it. Not at all like the mind
circling, ring upon ring—*I can't, I shouldn't, I shouldn't
have, I'll never again*—no end, no apparent ending. What I
meant was: as a suddenly wounded bird of prey, from a steep
and harder-by-the-moment-to-negotiate height descending.

THE SHORE

Don't be afraid— Don't go— Passenger me back to
*a land called neither Honeycomb nor Danger—*Yes,
that's what they kept whispering, as if in prayer (but
to what, or whom?), or at least sometimes whispering,
other times more loudly: *You're a memory   You're*
the future   You're a memory

                                as from a wilderness of
longing for something by now so clearly irretrievable
(we look back once, I think, if we're lucky—if
twice lucky, we never look back again), their bodies
meanwhile lifting, falling, sexual, like hammers, like
a hammer thrown up into and across where the sky
had begun—slowly, then more slowly—to seem
too wrecked enough already to sustain more damage.

THE NEED FOR DREAMING

As a scar commemorates what happened,
so is memory itself but a scar. As in: *Given*
hunger, which is endless only until it isn't, he
destroyed what he could. And then? —

So the lover enters the beloved — enters,
and withdraws; so a yellow-crested
night heron wades into view, then out:
useless? It gets harder to say. Like
signs of struggle in a field where nothing
stirs, the past can seem everywhere. I think
to be useless doesn't have to mean
not somehow mattering. Years now, and

still I can't stop collecting the strewn shells
of spent ammunition where I come across them;
carefully, I hold each up toward what's left of the light.

COMES THE FALL

But differently, the kind of bondage that's been
mostly sport—meaning competition—becoming force
of habit, and then just how it's been always: little
crack in the glass that regret blows sometimes

through, beyond it the branches and the foliage
that they hold indifferently aloft, each leaf a ribbed
sail that the wind catches, the way hunger
catches, the land falling away as the sea opens
out again into a loneliness that, often enough,

freedom also means—doesn't it? . . . As if
all this time you'd been dreaming. A dream
of horses. Two of them. Fitted with blinders. This,
the better life, the best way. Horses, and the present
future they kept thundering into . . .

MASTER AND SLAVE

For the longest time, he said nothing. I looked
through the glass at what he was looking at: brindled
dog shaking the rain free of herself in a field of flowers,
making the colors stir where, before, there'd been
a stillness like what precedes a dangerous undertow or
a choice that, for better—and worse—will change a life
forever.
    If you can't love everything, he said,
Try to love what, in the end, will matter. Not the dog,
doomed to fail, but the rain itself; the rain, getting
shaken . . . There are days when, almost, I think I know
what he meant by that. I can understand—I can at least
believe I do—his face, his mouth, that last time: for once,
unferocious; done with raging at his own regretlessness and confusion.

CLEAR, CLOUDLESS

Tonight—in the foundering night, at least,
of imagination, where what I don't in fact
believe anymore, all the same, is true—

the stars look steadily down upon me. I look
up, at the stars. Life as a recklessly fed bonfire
growing unexpectedly more reckless seems
neither the best nor worst of several choices
within reach, still. I wear on my head a crown

of feathers—among which, sure, I have had
my favorites. Fear, though, is the bluest feather,
and it is easily the bluest feather that the wind loves most.

ROSES

Where the shadows refuse equally to fend for
themselves and for the light without which
there would
               be no shadow. Where the world
as I'd thought I'd known it, once, stammers
blindfolded with a rough sash, trampling
the blood grass,
                    the mint with its spikes of
little purplish flowers—what stirs, what

doesn't . . . Where the land ends no differently
than it's ever had to, in a blue of sea, beside
which
          love lies deciduous, fast asleep, as,
with all the usual, to-be-pitied ambition
of the long restrained who believe they've
been at last
                set free—though they have not,
they'll never be—the waves shove closer.

NIGHT

Superfluous as blowflies to a carcass the lions
have had their sway with,

                    and the carcass rotting there,
a gift, into sweetness, to the part past sweetness—
forced surrender and, after that,

                          that slow dissolve
into nothingness to which nevertheless there's
a music that lingers still, ignore it or don't,
it keeps lingering anyway, song of risk,

                          song of

faintheartedness—

                    But by then, it was morning again.
We could see what it was to be at last forsaken—
not so much by others, as by what we'd come to
think of as our better selves, the part we'd

*

miss more, should it go away. And now that it
had, the departure seemed forever to have been at
once inevitable and obvious. It was as if we had
blinded ourselves unknowingly—and now we knew.
And truly then,
             we were frightened—alone with
what, rather than trying to escape the mind's grasp,
refused to leave it, instead kept changing its shape
inside it: now risk,
                now faintheartedness, now
a kind of youth again, now pleasure as the effacement
entirely of what, inside us, we couldn't bear
looking long at, no,
               not a moment longer . . . And

*

the world—that had seemed before so vast,
and canyoned—the world as body, and the body
beneath us, small, masterable, singing *I've been
unto myself a model for all darkness and all light,*
singing *I have given as a mirror gives, giving back
the night*—
        But it's morning, now. The blues
are various. The blacks are. The deaths are random.

For now, we're spared. The limbs of the trees
re-announce

themselves, stripped to a leaflessness
that we call ritual, though in nature there is nothing
of ritual, only repetition: the rain, falling; the blue
heron lifting itself up, into it, pulling seaward,
away; and

in that recurring picture of the mind
caught critiquing its finally less than pure reason,
God shutting his eyes,

dreaming,

clutching tightly
to his chest the snake—restored, forgiven—as it
hisses lullaby: *O my catacomb, drifting, my
drowse-in-honey-until-there's-nothing, nothing,
why be afraid, what are you*

so afraid of? That's

*

just a picture. Who's to say redemption won't
turn out to have been a matter of duration mostly,
of suffering for what we ourselves were free,
all along,

to call time enough? Against

a backdrop of boats, each moored at its prow, facing
into the wind the way boats tend to—which is not
resistance, not weakness either, just an absence

*

of choice—it's another morning. The restless choir
that any human life can be, sometimes, casts forth
all over again its double shadow: now risk, and now
faintheartedness—we're not what
                              either of us expected,
are we?—each one a form of disembodiment,
without the other.

ON HORSEBACK

More and more, I agree: a forced decision
is not a true one. To fuck; to forgive. As if
the two were the same — no, as when they
are the same. The hawk is neither more nor
less worth praising for the fact that it kills than
for the elegance with which it does so. The nights
are long, here. Nowhere a torch. No beacons,
either. Distortion works the only way it can. At
once both a thing that blinds and a form of blindness.

ALMOST TENDERLY

It had the heft of old armor—like a breastplate
of bronze; like a shield, on hinges. It swung apart
like a door. Inside it, the sea was visible—the sea
and, on the shore, a man: stripped; beaten. Very
gently—tenderly, almost—as if to the man, to
calm him, but in fact to no one, the sea was singing:
Here, in the deepening blue of our corruption, let

love be at least one corruption we chose together.
But the man said nothing. *Why not call restlessness
our crown, and our dominion,* sang the sea . . . But
the man was a brokenness like any other: moving,
until it fails to move—the way, over time, suffering
makes no difference. His wounds were fresh; still open.
Where the light fell on them, they flashed, like the sea.

TELL ME A STORY

Maybe this is the prettiest time for it, each tree
but a variation on the governing form, here,
a leaflessness more like death than sleep, less like
singing than remembering what it meant, once,
to sing—and the memory, enough. Though it seems
too early, already there are buds on the star magnolia—
so soft, they feel like a buck's first set of antlers,
just beginning to show . . . When I touch them,

something rises inside me, that I at first mistake
for gratitude, and then for regret. It descends, then
settles, like a flock of waterfowl on water, the particular
beauty that attends oblivion attending them also, in
their back-and-forthing, and even after that, when,
as I understand it, they'll have grown very still.

DARK ANGEL

Now that the festival of Saint Wish for It and It
Shall Be Yours is at last over, dying slowly
behind me, I've come down to the shore. Black
waves, silver on black . . . This time, I'll accept
what I'm given. I'll say I deserve it. Who
knows? Couldn't I
                    mean that, eventually?
Sure you will. Sure, he says, whispering as —
body first, the usual set of wings after (black
wings, silver on black) — he maneuvers into
the twilight as if into some small, crowded
room or, smaller, a dream of one, though it's
just me here, twilit in whatever room sea
and sky make, his
                    legs as he squats spreading
open: yes, the usual stuff findable, if you
want, between them — now destroy; now revive
for destruction . . . Dark Angel, I hate you, and —
And I love you like snow. Like snow caught
flying over open water from a fast-moving train.

AS IF LIT FROM BENEATH, AND TOSSING

They spoke into the night, the three of them, and then
through the night,
                agreeing at last,
                        forgetfulness was but a form
of imprecision, nothing more than that, meaning loyalty
is very like devotion —
                to be on fire, to burn,
to have been
                on fire — though they were not the same, and knew this,
even as they lay down together exhausted,
                        more still than a flooded
meadow, or the water inside it,
                or the black sky that the black water keeps,
and gives back.

GLORY ON

So there's a rustling in the grass that is not what
rustles from within the fir trees—unadorned, trans-
fixed, aromatic—so what. Show me a longing
that's got no history to it, that steep glide into
what it meant once, to have glided steeply, and I'll
show you belief as a thing that's touchable: go ahead,
touch it; try to . . . Brokenness, you do surprise me—
here I could have sworn I'd lost my taste for you,
you being an accident like all the others that, one
by one, constellate, first becoming a life, and then
as if the only one, as if no other were possible. Since
when does that make a world? Whose business
but mine is it if now, when I grieve, I grieve
this way: crown in hand, little flowers of gold?

MY BLUEST SHIRT

Now uselessness casts its shadowy ligature
across *If only*. Now—never mind how
briefly—conquest almost seems not to have,
from the start, been the only color,

                                each defeat
a stepping-stone across a stream whose
name, maybe, should have mattered more,

                      *

but didn't. It's late. It's dark out. Crush
of hollyhock and lantana, and flawed
intention. Bells, as if meant

                        to remind us. Clumsy
eloquence of a body faltering; fumbling rhythmically.
—Look at me. Little ocean, getting farther away.
Now I touch at once both everything and nothing.

OF THE RIPPLING SURFACE

The dragonflies are only the first thing. How they're
not what you think, or thought you would. Couldn't this,
too, be rescue? And then how, eventually, you start
forgetting to ask. The air hangs heavy with the smell
of catalpa trees
                    at last in bloom, the flowers themselves
tossing for once neither like gratitude nor one of those
many hard-to-pin-down-exactly forms of what they
used to call divine favor, but as when, with a patience
more human, it seems, than animal, the lion tears the doe's
body, as if forever,
                    steadily more open. There are ways
to be lost worse than this one. They can sway like suspicion—
like a river, as now. *Nothing was was nothing nothing was*
—that's the river, singing. Almost, you can see it. Even from here.

THE GRISTMILL

Creeping speedwell, wild thyme, yes, and—tamer of
trembling, persuading the hand to rest briefly, stay—the soft
moss where there still
               was some. Cries, as of rage crossed
with agony, that were only the gulls—though I was frightened
anyway—hovering in vain over what by then were ghost
herring, having run already, having spawned, then done
the whole thing, seaward,
                   backwards again. Not the pattern
of thinking, which is radial—a wheel, the light in its scattering,
water around where the diver falls, vanishes—but of that
gesture that begins as memory, which is a stillness, and then
becomes remembering: so relentless
                      it had seemed unstoppable,
Little Soul, Scantling, Scant, Little Heathen, as when to name
is to accuse also, *Tell me, what is hunger, tell what it means*
to have spent a life saying no to it, and emerged victorious.

AFTER WINNING THE WEST

They were what they'd always been—
perhaps inevitably. As a gift is several
things, yes, but it
                        isn't magic. Never
mind everywhere the light sort of
trembling, after. Soon enough, they'd
return
            to knowing this, and have to stop
mistaking themselves for what they did
and did not resemble: archers on the wall
of an Etruscan tomb, aiming
                                    at nothing,
each astride a creature by now bodiless
except for the hooves, barely visible,
that could stand for anything, why not
discipline,
                the stillness of it, just before
leaving the hard ground far behind?

SACRIFICE IS A DIFFERENT
ANIMAL ALTOGETHER

Wilderness. Bright cupola. Trimming the bittersweet and
raspberries along the marsh. Hands reddening easily in
the cold

of the air. The salt of it. The particular wakefulness
of pursuit-all-over-again. Yes. The rugged

tenderness required

*

to negotiate the delicate new growth of leaves. Tendrils. Little
invitations. Come here,

a moment. How the sailor can become
the ocean he'd meant only, he thought, to sail across. Closer.
No, the part

after that. One of us is going to have to say it first.

LIKE A LION

Fallopian, estranged somehow,
forgetless against a backdrop of plain
sky, the limbs of the trees
fail, and rally. Everywhere
the kinds of patterns that
should be breakable, but by now it's
been this way, it seems, forever. The wind

strikes. The wind dies down. To amplify
what's true past recognition—never mind
the cost . . . Hard to believe, though I
do believe it, that that's all
pleasure meant, once. Why not? *Why
not be totally changed
into fire, as they used to say,* I say
to no one. Cargo; rift; nostalgia; gold. I

fairly sway with my own aloneness, the only
half-blinding after all and, therefore,

not so unbearable flash of it, and the years
of my life, reducible to a shuddering
scant reflection in a body
of water nowhere visible, stir,
stir back.

CIVILIZATION

There's an art
    to everything. How
the rain means
    April and an ongoingness like
    that of song until at last

it ends. A centuries-old
    set of silver handbells that
once an altar boy swung,
    processing . . . *You're the same*
    wilderness you've always

been, slashing through briars,
    the bracken
of your invasive
    self. So he said,
    in a dream. But

the rest of it—all the rest—
   was waking: more often
than not, to the next
   extravagance. Two blackamoor
   statues, each mirroring

the other, each hoisting
   forever upward his burden of
hand-painted, carved-by-hand
   peacock feathers. *Don't*
   you know it, don't you know

I love you, he said. He was
   shaking. He said:
I love you. There's an art
   to everything. What I've
   done with this life,

what I'd meant not to do,
   or would have meant, maybe, had I
understood, though I have
   no regrets. Not the broken but
   still-flowering dogwood. Not

the honey locust, either. Not even
  the ghost walnut with its
non-branches whose
  every shadow is memory,
  memory . . . As he said to me

once, *That's all garbage*
  down the river, now. Turning,
but as the utterly lost—
  because addicted—do:
  resigned all over again. It

only looked, it—
  It must only look
like leaving. There's an art
  to everything. Even
  turning away. How

eventually even hunger
  can become a space
to live in. How they made
  out of shamelessness something
  beautiful, for as long as they could.

IMMACULATE EACH LEAF,
AND EVERY FLOWER

And everywhere the smaller birds again noising, filling
steadily all the cracks between spells of rain . . .

*

As if song could still mean something useful.

*

Or a kind of pleasure that, like forgiveness, came easily and,
summer storm that forgiveness is, passed quickly through.

*

And the undersong that has been your own voice saying *No—
No I'm not afraid.*

*

What we cannot do

What we cannot undo

All the work we must do

*

As for ruin—yes, but faintly.

*

The gray of doves. The gray of doves, in shadow.

THE LIFE YOU SAVE

After the pinefields, there's the marsh—you can
see it
    from here. *And after that?* History
ending; myth, as it starts
        to stir. *And after that?*

*

After that, just the turning back again. Nothing you
won't know, already:
        the pinefield; the marsh—

And the reeds, too? The reeds that grow there?

*

Yes,
    and the reeds that grow there: beautiful;
invasive; they jostle
        in the smallest wind.
Soon it will be as if nothing had ever happened.

HEAVEN AND EARTH

For days now, vertigo. Conqueror birds. Place where
suffering and a gift for it for a moment meet,
then go their separate ways. *I keep meaning to stop,
to wait for you.* Places where, all but untrackably, fear—
which is animal, and wild, and almost always
worth trusting—becomes cowardice: fear given
consciousness of a finite existence in the realm
of time—what exists,

                          and doesn't. Last night,
a stillness like that of moss; like permission when it's
not been given, yet not withheld exactly. Across the dark—
through it—the occasional handful of notes: someone
else out there, singing? or myself singing,
and the echoing after? I didn't know,

                                    or want to. A map
unfolding, getting folded back up again, seeming
sometimes—even as I held it—to be on fire:
It had seemed my life. What am I, that I should stand

so apart from my own happiness? The stars did
what they do, mostly: looked unbudging, transfixed,
like cattle asleep in a black pasture, all the restlessness
torn out of them, away, done with. I turn beneath them.

CATHEDRAL

And suddenly—strangely—there was also no fear, either.

As a horse in harness to what, inevitably, must break it.

No torch; no lantern—and yet no hiddenness, now. No hiding.

Leaves flew through where the wind sent them flying.

NOTES

The epigraph is from Schuyler's "The Crystal Lithium,"
Selected Poems, Farrar, Straus and Giroux, New York, 1988.

"Continuous Until We Stop": Karl Jaspers defines transition
as the zone of tragedy in "Basic Characteristics of the
Tragic in Tragedy," as it appears in *Tragedy: Vision and Form*,
Robert W. Corrigan (ed.), Harper and Row, New York, 1981.

"The Heat of the Sun": The breaking of willow
branches stood for parting in the T'ang Dynasty,
according to a footnote to a poem by Wang Wei in
Poems, Chang Yin-nan and Lewis C. Walmsley (trans.),
Charles E. Tuttle Company, Rutland, Vermont, 1958.

"My Bluest Shirt": "Bells, as if meant / to remind us"
paraphrases a line by Thomas Merton in *Thoughts
in Solitude*, The Noonday Press, New York, 1956.

"Like a Lion": "Why not be totally changed into fire?"
is attributed to Abbot Joseph, one of the Desert Fathers whose
sayings are included in *The Wisdom of the Desert*, Thomas
Merton (trans.), Shambhala Publications, Boston, 1994.

ACKNOWLEDGMENTS

Grateful acknowledgment is made to the editors of the following pub-
lications, in which these poems—sometimes in different versions—
originally appeared:

Barrow Street: "Clear, Cloudless"

Boulevard: "First Night at Sea," "Glory On," "Ransom"

Burnside Review: "Immaculate Each Leaf, and Every Flower"

Chicago Review: "After the Thunder, Before the Rain," "Roses"

The Drunken Boat: "Sacrifice Is a Different Animal Altogether"

Field: "Cathedral," "Continuous Until We Stop"

The Hampden-Sydney Poetry Review: "As If Lit
from Beneath, and Tossing," "The Gristmill"

The Harvard Advocate: "Comes the Fall"

The Kenyon Review: "Almost Tenderly," "The Heat of the Sun,"
"The Life You Save," "The Need for Dreaming," "Next Stop,
Arcadia," "Sky Coming Forward," "Tell Me a Story"

Meridian: "The Grass Not Being Flesh, Nor Flesh the Grass"

New England Review: "Dark Angel," "Night"

New Orleans Review: "Fascination"

The New Yorker: "Civilization"

Prairie Schooner: "The Shore"

A Public Space: "Through an Opening"

The Virginia Quarterly Review: "Master and Slave,"
"My Bluest Shirt," "Of the Rippling Surface"

West Branch: "On Horseback"

Witness: "Heaven and Earth"

The Yale Review: "After Winning the West," "Like a Lion"

*

"Night" was the Harvard University
Phi Beta Kappa poem for 2008.

"Heaven and Earth" also appeared in *The Best
American Poetry 2010*, Amy Gerstler and David
Lehman (eds.), Scribner, New York, 2010.